Y0-BZZ-402

# A STRANGER TO
# HEAVEN AND EARTH

# A STRANGER to HEAVEN and EARTH

Poems of Anna Akhmatova

Selected and Translated
by Judith Hemschemeyer

SHAMBHALA
Boston & London
1993

Shambhala Publications, Inc.
Horticultural Hall
300 Massachusetts Avenue
Boston, Massachusetts 02115

© 1983, 1984, 1985, 1986, 1987, 1988, 1989 by Judith
Hemschemeyer, reprinted by permission of Zephyr Press.
The translations were selected from *The Complete Poems of
Anna Akhmatova*, a bilingual, two-volume edition published
by Zephyr Press in 1990 and now out of print. A one-
volume English edition of *The Complete Poems of Anna
Akhmatova* is available from Zephyr Press, 13 Robinson St.,
Somerville, MA 02145.

All rights reserved. No part of this book may be
reproduced in any form or by any means,
electronic or mechanical, including photo-
copying, recording, or by any information
storage and retrieval system, without permission
in writing from the publisher.

9 8 7 6 5 4 3 2 1

First Shambhala Edition
Printed in Korea on acid-free paper
Distributed in the United States by Random House, Inc.,
and in Canada by Random House of Canada Ltd
See page 117 for Library of Congress
Cataloging-in-Publication data.

# Contents

# Translator's Preface

ANNA AKHMATOVA (born Anna Andreevna Gorenko) was one of the four major lyric poets of twentieth-century Russia. The other three, Boris Pasternak, Osip Mandelstam, and Marina Tsvetaeva, all died before her; Tsvetaeva was a suicide and Mandelstam was hunted down and hounded to death by Stalin. Pasternak died in 1960 and Akhmatova, who died in 1966, had a career that spanned more than 60 years.

Enormously resilient, intensely obsinate, she refused to emigrate, though she had many opportunities to do so. To her, being a Russian meant living in Russia no matter what its government did to her and her loved ones, and being a lyric poet meant writing the truth. Obviously, these two principles were destined to collide and they did, tragically, but it was Akhmatova's strength to be able to suffer tragedy, survive, and, somehow, write about it, over and over again.

By the time she was eleven years old, Anna Gorenko knew she would be a poet, even though the only poetry book in the house was a large volume of Nekrasov. By the age of 13, she was reading the poems of Verlaine, Baudelaire, and other French poets. When she started writing poetry, in her teens, her father told her he did not want his name associated with that trade, so she obliged by changing her surname to Akhmatova, the Tatar name of a maternal ancestor.

In 1903, when she was only 14, the young poet Nikolay Gumilyov began to court her desperately and she finally married him in 1910. Gumilyov introduced her to the literary society of Petersburg, which met in the fifth-floor apartment, called "The Tower," of Vyacheslav Ivanov, the reigning Symbolist poet.

In 1912, partly because he was exceedingly strong-willed, a born leader himself, and partly because he resented Ivanov's critique of one of his poems, Gumilyov, along with Sergey Gorodetsky, formed the Poets' Guild, a group of 15 young poets. At one of the Guild's early meetings, Gumilyov proposed that the members refute Symbolism and call themselves Adamists or Acmeists. Not all of the Guild members agreed, so the Acmeists, finally, numbered six: Gumilyov, Gorodetsky, Mandelstam, Narbut, Zenkevich, and Akhmatova.

What united them was a rejection of the

vague, the vatic, the ethereal and otherworldly aspects of Symbolism. Gorodetsky, Gumilyov, and Mandelstam all wrote manifestos defining Acmeism, proclaiming the need for a poetry of real experience and tangible objects. As Mandelstam said in his essay, "The Morning of Acmeism": "We do not wish to divert ourselves with a stroll in a 'forest of symbols,' because we have a more virgin, a denser forest—divine physiology, the infinite complexity of our dark organism." Since Mandelstam and Akhmatova were already writing and publishing poems based on the conviction that life on earth is a gift and the duty of the poet is to write about what Mandelstam called "the skin of the earth," it is probable, as Akhmatova conjectured later in her life, that the critical theory evolved from an already existing body of work.

Gumilyov's poems, mostly long, heroic-romantic narratives, were set in the wilds of Africa, where he had visited, or in imaginary lands. As he said in a letter to Akhmatova in 1913: "I never would have been able to guess that hearts can decay hopelessly from joy and fame, but then you would never have been able to concern yourself with research into the country of Gaul or understand, seeing the moon, that it is the diamond shield of the goddess of the warriors of Pallas."*

That astute comment defines the essence of Akhmatova. She was a poet of encounters; her strength was in observing her own actions and emotions, reporting as accurately as she could

---

*Quoted in *Anna Akhmatova, A Poetic Pilgrimage*, by Amanda Haight (Oxford University Press, 1976), p. 26.

what she was feeling, what she had done and said, what had been done and said to her. Of the Russian novelists, her favorite was Dostoevsky.

Unlike Pasternak and Tsvetaeva, who could write lyrically with only one consciousness, that of the poet, in the poem, Akhmatova almost always needed a "you." Because she was a beautiful, passionate woman, this "you" was most often the man who longed for her, the man she longed for, or someone who had betrayed or rejected her.

Akhmatova's early books, *Evening* (1912) and *Rosary* (1914), were instantly and wildly successful in pre-revolutionary Russia, especially with women. People flocked to the bohemian cabaret, the Stray Dog, to hear her recite her poetry, and her fans, who had memorized her books, used to "say the *Rosary*," one starting an Akhmatova poem and the others finishing it.

But Akhmatova's early lyrics had more than the refreshing frankness of her treatment of love to recommend them. Each one takes place in a real setting and contains real objects minutely observed, from the dilapidated well in the fields at her mother-in-law's estate to the high, ornamental balconies of the buildings of her beloved Petersburg. Like Colette, Akhmatova was passionately fond of nature and very good at using it in her art; nature observed almost always and with seeming unconscious ease carries emotional weight. Into these settings Akhmatova places her personae: sometimes the long-suffering peasant woman, sometimes the naive, betrayed peasant girl, but most often the Petersburg sophisticate hurting others and being hurt.

Akhmatova refused to glamorize love. In poem after poem, she insisted on looking her lover, her fellow-sufferer, straight in the eye. As she says in a poem of 1912:

. . .
> Don't look like that, that angry frown.
> I'm your beloved, I'm yours.
> Neither shepherdess nor queen
> And no longer a nun, I—
>
> In this everyday gray dress,
> On rundown heels . . .
> But, as before, the burning embrace,
> The same fear in enormous eyes.

. . .

It is ironic that Akhmatova's poetry, which rejected the image, so familiar in so-called love poetry, of woman as either virgin on a pedestal or whore, should be criticized according to these same tired, clichéd misconceptions of womanhood. It is equally ironic that Akhmatova, a psychological pioneer in the writing of lyric poetry, should, from the Twenties on, have been considered hopelessly old-fashioned by Soviet critics.

But that is exactly what happened. In September 1921, in a lecture entitled "Two Russias," Korney Chukovsky described Akhmatova as "a nun who crosses herself as she kisses her beloved" (Haight, p. 69). Although he went on to say that he envisioned a Russia enriched both by Akhmatova's poetry of "prerevolutionary culture" and Mayakovsky's poetry of the "present revolutionary age," other critics pounced on this phrase. Eikhenbaum, a Formalist critic, said that Akhmatova's heroine, "half harlot burning with passion, half mendicant nun able to pray to God for forgiveness, was paradoxical, or more correctly, contradictory" (Haight, 72). The Marxist critic Lelevich, using the same phrase, pronounced her poetry as unworthy of consideration in a revolutionary Communist society.

By the time of Chukovsky's speech in 1921, Gumilyov, from whom Akhmatova was already divorced, had been accused of taking part in a counter-revolutionary plot and executed. For Akhmatova, the Terror had begun.

In a country where the government could, and increasingly did, imprison and murder millions of its citizens, where everyone was in danger all the time, the ordinary bonds between people—love, friendship, kinship, trust, shared cultural assumptions and interests—broke down and dissolved and the only shared emotion was fear. In one of her early lyrics, Akhmatova had compared love to a hangman. Now the government was the hangman and the "you" she addressed her poems to might at any moment be liquidated or had perhaps already perished.

Nadezhda Mandelstam, in her two-volume memoir, *Hope Against Hope* and *Hope Abandoned* (Athenaeum, 1970 and 1974), details this tragic period from 1921 to the death of Stalin in 1953. She said that at one time in the Thirties, she was reduced to trusting only two people on earth, her husband and Akhmatova.

From 1925 until 1940, there was an unofficial ban on the publication of Akhmatova's poetry. Akhmatova concentrated on scholarship, immersing herself in her critical studies of Pushkin. But in 1935, following the arrest of Nikolay Punin, the man she was living with, and Lev Gumilyov, her son, she began to compose the 15-part poetry and prose cycle *Requiem*. Not daring to write it down, she recited various parts to friends, including Lidiya Chukovskaya (Korney Chukovsky's daughter), who memorized and reassembled them. *Requiem*, a tribute to the ordeal of the victims of the Terror and the women who waited in the prison lines hoping to get word of them, is based on her own experience in Leningrad, where Lev was imprisoned for 17 months. In this great cycle, the "you" becomes all Russians imprisoned and tortured by their own government. *Requiem* was finally published in the Soviet Union in April 1987, in the journal *Novy mir* and was included in a book of her poems, *Anna Akhmatova: Ya—golos vash . . . (Anna Akhmatova: I am your voice . . . ;* Moscow, 1989) and in subsequent editions of her work.

Akhmatova wrote other, publishable, poems during the war, including "Courage," which was recited everywhere in Russia. She became a symbol of stoic endurance and, during the siege of Leningrad, was called on by the government to give a radio speech to the heroic women of that city. Then, in November 1941, she was evacuated to Moscow and from there to the Central Asian city of Tashkent.

While in Tashkent she wrote a play about a nightmare-like show trial; it was performed once, then burnt, as were some poems she feared might be used against her son, whose whereabouts she didn't know. She also finished the first two parts of *Poem Without a Hero,* a long poem set at a masked ball in 1913 Petersburg on the eve of World War I. *Poem Without a Hero* obsessed her for the rest of her life. She wrote poems to it begging it to stop tormenting her; she changed it again and again, adding sections, eliminating others, deliberately using ellipses the way Pushkin, whose works were also censored, had had to do. One thing is constant, however, the tone of guilt and the premonition of the disasters that befell Petersburg and Akhmatova's whole generation.

In 1945, Akhmatova returned to Leningrad from Tashkent, giving a reading at the Moscow Polytechnic Museum on her way. By now, thanks to her wartime poems as well as her early books, she was the most popular poet in Russia and was applauded so enthusiastically that it frightened her. She knew that to draw attention to herself in any way was dangerous. Her fears were borne out.

In 1946, as a result of this tumultuous reception and because of a visit paid to her by Isaiah Berlin, she was expelled from the Union of Soviet Writers and viciously denounced by Andrey Zhdanov, who accused her of poisoning the minds of Soviet youth. Zhdanov, Stalin's cultural watchdog, used the criticism of the Twenties against Akhmatova, calling her "half nun, half harlot." However, Akhmatova was accustomed to disaster and she bore Zhdanov's scurrilous attack with equanimity.

Then, in 1949, Lev Gumilyov was arrested again. Akhmatova tried to help him by writing a cycle of poems praising Stalin and the regime. Lev was finally released in 1956 and the last decade of Akhmatova's life, on the surface at least, became somewhat easier. She was given the use of a tiny summer house and some translating work and allowed to travel abroad twice to receive literary awards. And she wrote; right up to the end of her life she was writing fresh, powerful poems. She had, in spite of the repressions, the deaths, and the betrayals, found a "you" again. Often now, the "you" was dead and the encounter was a non-meeting instead of a meeting, but the power of Akhmatova's memory for physical details and gestures never failed her. One of her last dated poems, February 1965, written when she was 75, is a tender poem about innocent love:

So we lowered our eyes,
Tossing the flowers on the bed,
We didn't know until the end,
What to call one another.
We didn't dare until the end
To utter first names,
As if, nearing the goal, we slowed our steps
On the enchanted way.

# Something in the World
## Called Love

You won't divine it immediately,
. . . . . . . . . . . . . . . . . . . the infection,
The one, as they say tenderly,
From which people die.
The first sign—a strange cheerfulness,
As if you had drunk an intoxicating potion,
And the second—grief, such grief,
That, exhausted, you can't breathe.
But the third—is the surest sign:
If your heart often skips a beat,
And the candles glow in your misty gaze,
This means that tomorrow you will meet

. . .

From the 1910s

When you're drunk it's so much fun—
Your stories don't make sense.
An early fall has strung
The elms with yellow flags.

We've strayed into the land of deceit
And we're repenting bitterly,
Why then are we smiling these
Strange and frozen smiles?

We wanted piercing anguish
Instead of placid happiness . . .
I won't abandon my comrade,
So dissolute and mild.

1911
Paris

4

In the corner an old man resembling a ram
Is poring over *Figaro*.
In my hand an idle pen,
It's still too early to go home.

I ordered you to leave.
Your eyes told me everything instantly . . .
The floor is thick in sawdust
And the half-moon hall smells of alcohol

And this is youth—that glorious time
. . . . . . . . . . . . . . . . . . . .
I should have hanged myself yesterday
Or thrown myself under a train today.

Spring 1911
Paris

5

One heart isn't chained to another,
If you want to—leave!
There's lots of happiness in store
For one who's free.

I'm not weeping, I'm not complaining,
Happiness is not for me.
Don't kiss me, I am weary—
Death will kiss me.

Days of gnawing tedium endured
With the winter snow.
Why, oh why should you
Be better than the one I chose?

Spring 1911

HE LOVED . . .

He loved three things in life:
Evensong, white peacocks
And old maps of America.
He hated it when children cried,
He hated tea with raspberry jam
And women's hysterics.
. . . And I was his wife.

November 9, 1910
Kiev

They didn't bring me a letter today:
He forgot to write, or he went away;
Spring is like a trill of silver laughter,
Boats are rocking in the bay.
They didn't bring me a letter today . . .

He was still with me just recently,
So much in love, affectionate and mine,
But that was white wintertime.
Now it is spring, and spring's sadness is
    poisonous.
He was still with me just recently . . .

I listen: the light, trembling bow of a violin,
Like the pain before death, beats, beats,
How terrible that my heart will break
Before these tender lines are complete . . .

1912

They didn't bring me a letter today:
He forgot to write, or he went away;
Spring is like a trill of silver laughter,
Boats are rocking in the bay,
They didn't bring me a letter today.

Darling, don't crumple my letter,
Read it through, my friend, to the end.
I've had enough of being unknown,
The strange one on your path.

And when we had cursed each other,
Passionate, white hot,
We still didn't understand
How small the earth can be for two people,
And that memory can torment savagely.
The anguish of the strong—a wasting
    disease!
And in the endless night the heart learns
To ask: Oh, where is my departed lover?
And when, through waves of incense,
The choir thunders, exulting and threatening,
Those same eyes, inescapable,
Stare sternly and stubbornly into the soul.

1909

# Confusion

### 1

It was stifling in the burning light,
And his glances—like rays.
I merely shuddered: this one
Could tame me.
He bowed—he will say something . . .
The blood drained from my face.
Let love be the gravestone
Lying on my life.

### 2

Don't you love me, don't you want to look
    at me?
Oh, how handsome you are, damn you!
And I can no longer fly,

I who was winged from childhood.
A mist clouds my eyes,
Things and faces merge and flow,
And there is only the red tulip,
The tulip in your buttonhole.


3

As simple civility demands,
You approached me, you smiled,
And half tenderly, half lazily,
With a kiss you brushed my hand—
And the eyes of mysterious, ancient faces
Gazed at me . . .

Ten years of cries and trepidation,
All my sleepless nights,
I put into one quiet word
And I uttered it—in vain.
You left and once again my soul became
Empty and serene.

1913

One would not mistake true tenderness
For this. It is quiet.
In vain you solicitously wrap
My shoulders and my breast with furs.
And in vain you utter respectful words
About the first love.
How well I know those persistent,
Unsatisfied glances of yours!

December 1913

Tsarskoye Selo

I have a certain smile:
Like this, a barely visible movement of the
   lips.
I am keeping it for you—
Love gave it to me, after all.
Never mind that you are insolent and evil,
Never mind that you love others.
Before me is the golden lectern,
And beside me is my gray-eyed bridegroom.

1913

How many demands the beloved can make!
The woman discarded, none.
How glad I am that today the water
Under the colorless ice is motionless.

And I stand—Christ help me!—
On this shroud that is brittle and bright,
But save my letters
So that our descendants can decide,

So that you, courageous and wise,
Will be seen by them with greater clarity.
Perhaps we may leave some gaps
In your glorious biography?

Too sweet is earthly drink,
Too tight the nets of love.
Sometime let the children read
My name in their lesson book,

And on learning the sad story,
Let them smile slyly . . .
Since you've given me neither love nor peace,
Grant me bitter glory.

1913

Darling, don't crumple my letter,
Read it through, my friend, to the end.
I've had enough of being unknown,
The strange one on your path.

Don't look like that, that angry frown.
I'm your beloved, I'm yours.
Neither shepherdess nor queen
And no longer a nun, I—

In this everyday gray dress,
On rundown heels . . .
But, as before, the burning embrace,
The same fear in enormous eyes.

Darling, don't crumple my letter,
Don't cry over intimate lies.
Put it in your poor old knapsack,
There, at the very bottom, let it lie.

1912
Tsarskoye Selo

I led my lover out to the hall,
I stood in a golden haze.
From a nearby bell tower
Solemn sounds flowed.
A throwaway! Invented word—
Am I really a note or a flower?
But eyes already gaze bleakly
Into the darkening mirror.

1913
Tsarskoye Selo

I will leave your white house and tranquil
   garden.
Let life be empty and bright.
You, and only you, I shall glorify in my
   poems,
As a woman has never been able to do.
And you remember the beloved
For whose eyes you created this paradise,
But I deal in rare commodities—
I sell your love and tenderness.

1913
Tsarskoye Selo

Weak is my voice, but my will isn't
   weakening,
It's even become easier for me without love.
The sky is sublime, a mountain wind is
   blowing,
And my thoughts are pure.

Insomnia, my nightnurse, is visiting
   elsewhere,
I'm not brooding by a cold hearth,
And the crooked hand of the tower clock
Doesn't look like the arrow of death.

How the past loses power over the heart!
Liberation is at hand. I forgive everything.
I'm keeping track of a sunbeam running up
   and down
The first moist ivy of spring.

Spring 1912

Memory of love, you are painful!
I must sing and burn in your smoke,
But for others—you're just a flame
To warm a cooling soul.

To warm a sated body,
They needed my tears . . .
For this, Lord, I sang,
For this I received love's communion!

Let me drink some kind of poison
That will make me mute,
And turn my infamous fame
Into radiant oblivion.

July 18, 1914
Slepnyovo

There is a sacred boundary between those
   who are close,
And it cannot be crossed by passion or
   love—
Though lips fuse in dreadful silence
And the heart shatters to pieces with love.

Friendship is helpless here, and years
Of exalted and ardent happiness,
When the soul is free and a stranger
To the slow languor of voluptuousness.

Those who strive to reach it are mad, and
   those
Who reach it—stricken by grief . . .
Now you understand why my heart
Does not beat faster under your hand.

May 1915
Petersburg

Somewhere there is a simple life and a
    world,
Transparent, warm and joyful . . .
There at evening a neighbor talks with a girl
Across the fence, and only the bees can hear
This most tender murmuring of all.

But we live ceremoniously and with difficulty
And we observe the rites of our bitter
    meetings,
When suddenly the reckless wind
Breaks off a sentence just begun—

Do I not talk to you
With the screech of birds of prey?
Do I not stare into your eyes
From the dull white page?

At the window beating its wings
Is the white, white Day of the Holy Ghost

But not for anything would we exchange this splendid
    splendid
Granite city of fame and calamity,
The wide rivers of glistening ice,
The sunless, gloomy gardens,
And, barely audible, the Muse's voice.

        June 23, 1915
        Slepnyovo

We don't know how to say good-bye—
We keep wandering arm in arm.
Twilight has begun to fall,
You are pensive and I keep still.

Let's go into a church—we will watch
A funeral, christenings, a marriage service,
Without looking at each other, we will leave
   . . .
What's wrong with us?

Or let's sit on the trampled snow
Of the graveyard, sighing lightly,
And with your walking stick you'll outline
   palaces
Where we will be together always.

The twenty-first. Night. Monday.
The outlines of the capital are in mist.
Some idler invented the idea
That there's something in the world called love.

And from laziness or boredom,
Everyone believed it and here is how they
    live:
They anticipate meetings, they fear partings
And they sing the songs of love.

But the secret will be revealed to the others,
And a hush will fall on them all . . .
I stumbled on it by accident
And since then have been somehow unwell.

1917
Petersburg

The sky sows a fine rain
On the lilacs in bloom.
At the window beating its wings
Is the white, white Day of the Holy Ghost.

By today at the latest, my love
Should have returned from across the sea.
I keep dreaming of the distant coast,
Rocks, towers and sand.

I ascend one of those towers,
Meeting the light . . .
But in this country of fens and ploughed
   fields,
There's no trace of a tower.

I will just sit on the threshold,
There the shadow is still dense.
White, white Day of the Holy Ghost,
Dispel my uneasiness!

May 1916
Slepnyovo

I dream of him less often now, thank God,
He doesn't appear everywhere anymore.
Fog lies on the white road,
Shadows start to run along the water.

And the ringing goes on all day.
Over the endless expanse of ploughed fields,
Ever louder sound the bells
From Jonah's Monastery far away.

I am clipping today's wilted branches
From the lilac bushes;
On the ramparts of the ancient fortress,
Two monks stroll.

Revive for me, who cannot see,
The familiar, comprehensible, corporeal
    world.
The heavenly king has already healed my
    soul
With the peace of unlove, icy cold.

1912
Kiev

In every twenty-four hours there is one
That is confused and anxious.
I talk out loud to this anguish
Without opening my drowsy eyes,
And it beats on, like the blood,
Like warm breath,
Like happy love,
Calculating and malicious.

1917

Over the snowdrift's hard crust
Into your white, mysterious house,
We walk in tender silence,
Both hushed.
And sweeter to me than all songs sung
Is this dream fulfilled,
The gentle clinking of your spurs
And the swaying of branches we've brushed.

January 1917

You are always novel and mysterious,
I am more submissive with each day.
But your love, oh my exacting lover,
Is a trial by iron and fire.

You forbid singing and smiling,
And praying you forbade long ago.
As long as we don't separate,
Let everything else go!

Thus, a stranger to heaven and earth,
I live and no longer sing,
It's as if you cut off my wandering soul
From both paradise and hell.

December 1917

Why do you wander restlessly?
Why do you stare breathlessly?
Surely you comprehend: our two souls
Have been firmly welded into one.

You will be, you will be comforted by me
In a way no one could dream,
And when you wound with an angry word—
You yourself will feel the pain.

December 1921
Petersburg

He whispers: "I'm not sorry
For loving you this way—
Either be mine alone
Or I will kill you."
It buzzes around me like a gadfly,
Incessantly, day after day,
This same boring argument,
Your black jealousy.
Grief smothers—but not fatally,
The wide wind dries my tears
And cheerfulness begins to soothe,
To smooth out this troubled heart.

February 1922

Oh, life without tomorrow's day!
I detect treason in every word,
And the star of waning love
Rises for me.

To vanish like that, imperceptibly,
Almost unaware of this encounter.
But again it's night. And once more,
To kiss those shoulders in moist languor.

I was never dear to you,
You disgust me. But the torment drags on,
And love, like a criminal,
Languishes, brimming with evil.

Just like a brother. You are silent, enraged.
But if our eyes should meet—
By the heavens I swear to you,
Granite would melt in that heat.

August 29, 1921

38

Ah—you thought I'd be the type
You could forget,
And that praying and sobbing, I'd throw
   myself
Under the hooves of a bay.

Or I would beg from the witches
Some kind of root in charmed water
And send you a terrible gift—
My intimate, scented handkerchief.

Damned if I will. Neither by glance nor
   by groan
Will I touch your cursed soul,

But I vow to you by the garden of angels,
By the miraculous icon I vow
And by the fiery passion of our nights—
I will never return to you.

July 1921
Petersburg

## PARTING

I

Not weeks, not months—years
We spent parting. And now finally
The chill of real freedom
And the gray garland above the temples.

No more treasons, no more betrayals,
And you won't be listening till dawn,
As the stream of evidence
Of my perfect innocence flows on.

1940

2

And, as always happens in the days of final
    rupture,
The ghost of the first days knocked at our
    door,
And in burst the silver willow
In all its gray, branching splendor.

To us, frenzied, disdainful and bitter,
Not daring to raise our eyes from the
    ground,
A bird began to sing in a voice of rapture
About how much we cherished one another.

September 25, 1944

## Farewell Song

I didn't laugh and didn't sing,
I kept silent all day,
And above all I wanted to be with you
From the very beginning:
The delicious delirium
Of the first lighthearted spat,
And the silent, stale, hasty
Last repast.

1959

## FRAGMENT

See where you're obliged to wander,
Shade from the shadows, strange bride!
Really, couldn't you find
A better place to stroll?
Approaching winter has already meandered
   here,
Lightly powdering the furrowed fields,
Inadvertently turning the distance
Into impenetrable haze.
Did it really seem bad to you
There by the dark green sea,
That, submitting to terrible fate,
You didn't argue, you agreed?
You, the most forbidden of roses,
You, crowned twice to reign,

Here the first frost will kill you.

. . . . . . . . . . . . . . . . . . . . . . . . .

The crooked cupola,
Puddles, geese and the sound of the train,
And a poplar charred by the moon
Stretches its crucified arms to heaven.

. . . . . . . . . . . . . . . . . . . . . . . . . . .

The stars, those magical emeralds,
And underfoot, rustling heaps
Of rusty, rotting, fragrant leaves.

. . . . . . . . . . . . . . . . . . . . . . .

. . . . . . . . . . . . . . . . . . . . . . .

But she is silent, spellbound, this shade,
Not answering me with one word.

# I Am Not with Those Who
# Abandoned Their Land

When in suicidal anguish
The nation awaited its German guests,
And the stern spirit of Byzantium
Had fled from the Russian Church,
When the capital by the Neva,
Forgetting her greatness,
Like a drunken prostitute
Did not know who would take her next,
A voice came to me. It called out comfort-
    ingly,
It said, "Come here,
Leave your deaf and sinful land,
Leave Russia forever.
I will wash the blood from your hands,
Root out the black shame from your heart,
With a new name I will conceal
The pain of defeats and injuries."

But calmly and indifferently,
I covered my ears with my hands,
So that my sorrowing spirit
Would not be stained by those shameful
   words.

                        Autumn 1917

## PETROGRAD, 1919

And confined to this savage capital,
We have forgotten forever
The lakes, the steppes, the towns,
And the dawns of our great native land.
Day and night in the bloody circle
A brutal languor overcomes us . . .
No one wants to help us
Because we stayed home,
Because, loving our city
And not winged freedom,
We preserved for ourselves
Its palaces, its fire and water.

A different time is drawing near,
The wind of death already chills the heart,
But the holy city of Peter
Will be our unintended monument.

I am not with those who abandoned
	their land
To the lacerations of the enemy.
I am deaf to their coarse flattery,
I won't give them my songs.

But to me the exile is forever pitiful,
Like a prisoner, like someone ill.
Dark is your road, wanderer,
Like wormwood smells the bread of
	strangers.

But here, in the blinding smoke of the
	conflagration
Destroying what's left of youth,
We have not deflected from ourselves
One single stroke.

And we know that in the final accounting,
Each hour will be justified . . .
But there is no people on earth more tearless
More simple and more full of pride.

July 1922
Petersburg

You are no longer among the living,
You cannot rise from the snow.
Twenty-eight bayonets,
Five bullets.

A bitter new shirt
For my beloved I sewed.
The Russian earth loves, loves
Droplets of blood.

August 16, 1921

Here the most beautiful girls fight
For the honor of marrying executioners.
Here they torture the righteous at night
And wear down the untamable with hunger.

1924

And into the windows of my room
The northern breezes often fly . . .

And he shreds the carpet
With his short spurs.
Now, that meek smile
Won't appear in the mirrors.

It would be so easy to abandon this life,
To burn down painlessly and unaware,
But it is not given to the Russian poet
To die a death so pure.

A bullet more reliably throws open
Heaven's boundaries to the soul in flight,
Or hoarse terror with a shaggy paw can,
As if from a sponge, squeeze out the heart's
    life.

1925

Why did you poison the water
And mix dirt with my bread?
Why did you turn the last freedom
Into a den of thieves?
Because I didn't jeer
At the bitter death of friends?
Because I remained true
To my sorrowing motherland?
So be it. Without hangman and scaffold
A poet cannot exist in the world.
Our lot is to wear the hair shirt,
To walk with a candle and to wail.

1935

And I am not at all a prophet,
My life is pure as a stream.
I simply don't feel like singing
To the sound of prison keys.

1930s

To the New Year! To new bitterness!
See how he dances, mischievous child,
Over the smoky Baltic Sea,
Bowlegged, hunchbacked and wild.
What kind of fate has he
For those beyond the torture chamber?
They have gone to the fields to die.
Shine on them, heavenly stars!
Earthly bread, beloved eyes,
Are no longer theirs to see.

January 1940

## STANZAS

Sagittarius moon. Beyond the Moscow
  River. Night.
Like a religious procession the hours of
  Holy Week go by.
I had a terrible dream. Is it possible
That no one, no one, no one can help me?

You had better not live in the Kremlin, the
  Preobrazhensky Guard was right;
The germs of the ancient frenzy are still
  swarming here:
Boris Godunov's wild fear, and all the Ivans'
  evil spite,
And the Pretender's arrogance—instead of
  the people's rights.

1940

*In the forest the trees vote.*
                N. Z.


And here, in defiance of the fact
That death is staring me in the eye—
Because of your words
I am voting *for:*
For a door to become a door,
A lock—a lock once more,
For this morose beast within my breast
To become a heart. But the thing is,
That we are all fated to learn
What it means not to sleep for three years,
What it means to find out in the morning
About those who have died in the night.

                        1940

With the rabble in a ditch
By the pub,
With the prisoners on the bench
Of the truck.

Under the thick fog
Over the Moscow River,
With the father-Ataman
In a taut noose.

I was with all of them,
With these and with those,
But now I remain
All by myself, alone.

Autumn 1946

*. . . And the deserts of mute squares,*
*Where people were executed before dawn.—*

I. Annensky

Everyone left and no one returned,
Only, true to the promise of love,
My latest, at least you looked back
To see the whole sky in blood.
The house was cursed, and cursed was
    my trade;
Uselessly, a tender song rang out
And I didn't dare raise my eyes
To my terrible fate.
They defiled the immaculate Word,
They trampled the sacred utterance,
So that with the sicknurses of Thirty-Seven
I could mop the bloody floor.

They separated me from my only son,
They tortured my friends in prisons,
They surrounded me with an invisible
   stockade
Of well-coordinated shadowing.
They rewarded me with a muteness
That curses the whole cursed world,
They force-fed me with scandal,
They made me drink poison.
And taking me to the very edge,
For some reason they left me there.
I would rather, as one of the city's "crazies,"
Be wandering through the dying squares.

                End of the 1940s

# SHARDS

*You cannot leave your mother an orphan.*

—Joyce

### I

For me, deprived of fire and water,
Separated from my only son . . .
Being on the infamous scaffold of misfortune
Is like being beneath the canopy of a throne

. . .

### II

How well he's succeeded, this fierce debater,
All the way to the Yenisey plains . . .
To you he's a vagabond, rebel, conspirator—
To me he is—an only son.

### III

Seven thousand and three kilometers . . .
Don't you hear your mother's call
In the north wind's frightful howl?
Cooped up, surrounded by adversity,
You grow wild there, you grow savage—you
    are dear,
You are the last and the first, you—are ours.
Over my Leningrad grave
Spring wanders indifferently.

## FESTIVE SONG

Under the embroidered tablecloth,
   No table to be seen.
I was not mother to the poems—
   But stepmother.
Ach! White paper,
   Straight row of lines!
How many times I've watched
   Them burn.
Maimed by gossip,
   Beaten with bludgeons,
Stamped, stamped
   With the convict's brand.

1955

Others go off with their loved ones—
I don't look after them with envy.
I've been sitting alone in the prisoner's dock
For almost half a century,
Surrounded by quarrels and crowds
And the cloying smell of ink.
It's like something invented by Kafka
And played by Chaplin.
And in these momentous arguments,
As in the tenacious embrace of sleep,
Three generations of juries
Decided: "She is guilty."
The faces of the guards change,
The sixth procurator has a heart attack . . .
And somewhere heaven's huge space
Darkens with heat,
And a whole summer of loveliness

Strolls on that shore . . .
I can't even imagine
That blessed "somewhere" anymore
I've been deafened by shouted curses,
I've worn out my prisoner's jacket.
Am I really more guilty than anyone
Who ever lived on this planet?

Middle of the 1950s

This is neither old nor new,
Nothing like a fairy tale.
Just as they cursed Otryopov and Pugachev,
For thirteen years they have been cursing me.

. . . . . . . . . . . . . . . . . . . . and cruelly,
Unyielding as granite.
From Libava to Vladivostok
The never-ending anathema rings out.

1959

No, we didn't suffer together in vain,
Without hopes of even drawing a breath.
We took an oath, we voted—
And quietly followed our path.
Not in vain did I remain pure,
Like a candle before the Lord,
Grovelling with you at the feet
Of the bloody puppet-executioner.
No, not under the vault of alien skies
And not under the shelter of alien wings—
I was with my people then,
There, where my people, unfortunately, were.

1961

## MASQUERADE CHATTER

And in an ordinary envelope,
Under the heading general death,
Was a full list,
Not a cryptogram to be deciphered,
But the impassive base
Of the invisible stream of nonlife.

March 1961

## To the Defenders of Stalin

There are those who shouted: "Release
Barabbas for us on this feast,"
Those who ordered Socrates to drink poison
In the bare, narrow prison.

They are the ones who should pour this
        drink
Into their own innocently slandering mouths,
These sweet lovers of torture,
Experts in the manufacture of orphans.

(1962)

The Lord Has Taught Us to Forgive

I wept and repented.
If only thunder would burst from the skies!
My heavy heart was exhausted
In your inhospitable house.
I know the unendurable pain,
The shame of the road back . . .
Terrible, terrible, to return
To the unloved one, the silent one.
If I bend over him, beautifully dressed,
Necklaces ringing—
He'll only ask: "My incomparable beauty!
Where were you praying for me?"

1911

## CONFESSION

Having forgiven me my sins, he fell silent.
In the violet dusk candles sputtered,
And a dark prayer stole
Covered my head and my shoulders.

Isn't that the voice that said: "Maiden!
    Arise . . ."
My heart beats faster, faster.
The touch, through the cloth,
Of a hand absently making the sign of
    the cross.

                    1911
                    Tsarskoye Selo

As if with a huge, heavy hammer,
They have smashed my frail breast.
Though the cost be shining gold—
Just once, just this once let me rest!
Just to lift one's head from the pillow
To see the wide pond again,
To see, once again, how over the tops
Of the gray firs the storm clouds swim.
I can stand anything: despair and pain,
Even sharp pity. Just don't place
Your dusty cloak of repentance
On my face.

Autumn 1911

For a long time I stood at Hell's heavy
   gates,
But Hell was dark and still . . .
Oh, even the Devil had no need of me,
Where then, shall I go? . .

December 23, 1910

Tsarskoye Selo

You gave me a difficult youth.
So much sadness in my path.
How can such a barren soul
Bear gifts to You?
Flattering fate
Sings a long song of praise.
Lord! I am negligent,
Your stingy servant.
Neither a rose nor a blade of grass
Will I be in my Father's garden.
I tremble at every mote of dust,
Before the words of any dunce.

December 19, 1912

Dying, I am tormented by immortality.
There's a low-hanging cloud of dusty haze
        . . .
Let there be naked red devils,
Let there be vats of stinking pitch.

Crawl up to me, play your tricks,
Your threats from antiquated books,
Only leave me my memory,
Only, at the last gasp, my memory.

So that you won't be a stranger to me
In the agonizing line,
I am ready to pay a hundredfold
For a smile and for a dream.

The hour of death, bowing, slakes my thirst
With clear, corrosive lye.
And people come and bury
My body and my voice.

1912
Tsarskoye Selo

You know, I languish in captivity,
Praying to the Lord for death.
But I remember, to the point of pain,
Tver's barren, meager earth.

The crane on the decrepit well,
Over it, boiling, the clouds,
In the field a creaking little gate,
And the smell of wheat, and weariness.

And those pale expanses,
Where even the voice of the wind is weak,
And the condemning way
Those quiet, sunburnt peasant women look
   at me.

Autumn 1913

Noiselessly they walked about the house,
No longer expecting anything.
They led me to the sick man
And I didn't recognize him.

He said: "Now praise God—"
And sank deeper into thought.
"I should have been on my way long ago,
I was only waiting for you.

You trouble me so much in my delirium,
I cherish each one of your words.
Tell me: can you not forgive?"
And I replied: "I can."

It seemed as if the walls shone
From floor to ceiling.
On the silken counterpane
Lay his shriveled hand.

And his arched, predatory profile
Became horribly heavy and coarse,
And there was no audible breath
From his dark, gnawed mouth.

But suddenly the last strength
Lit up his blue eyes:
"It's good that you forgive,
You weren't always so kind."

And his face became younger,
I recognized him again
And I said: "Lord God,
Gather your servant in."

July 1914
Slepnyovo

## PRAYER

Give me bitter years of sickness,
Suffocation, insomnia, fever,
Take my child and my lover,
And my mysterious gift of song—
This I pray at your liturgy
After so many tormented days,
So that the stormcloud over darkened Russia
Might become a cloud of glorious rays.

May 1915
Day of the Holy Ghost
Petersburg

And the burdocks stand shoulder high
And the forest of dense nettles sings . . .

Already beyond the judgment of earthly laws,
I, like a criminal, am still drawn there.

He didn't mock me, he didn't praise,
As friends would have, and enemies.
He only left me his soul
And said: Look after it.

And one thing troubles me:
If he dies now,
God's archangel will come to me
For his soul.

How then will I conceal it,
Keep it a secret from God?
This soul, which sings and cries,
Ought to be in His paradise.

July 1915

Under an oaken slab in the churchyard
I will sleep quietly,
You, darling, will come running
To visit Mama on Sunday—
Across the stream and along the rise,
Leaving the grownups far behind,
From far away, my sharp-sighted boy,
You will recognize my cross.
I know you won't be able
To remember much about me, little one:
I didn't scold you, I didn't hold you,
I didn't take you to Communion.

1915

And in the Kievian church of Divine
   Wisdom,
On my knees before the solium I bowed
   to you—
That your road be mine
No matter where it winds.
The golden angels heard
And even Yaroslav in his white sepulcher.
How the simple words of the dove hover
Even now in the sunny cupolas.
And if I weaken, I dream of an icon,
And the nine steps leading up to it,
And in the terrible voice of Sophia's bell
I hear the voice of your uneasiness.

1915

Ah! It's you again. Not as an enamoured
  youth
But as a husband, daring, stern, inflexible,
You enter this house and look at me.
My soul is frightened by the lull before the
  storm.
You ask what I have done with you,
Entrusted to me forever by love and fate.
I have betrayed you. And to have to
  repeat—
Oh, if only you'd get tired of it!
This is how a dead man speaks, disturbing
  his murderer's sleep,
This is how the angel of death waits by the
  bed of the dying.
Forgive me now. The Lord has taught us to
  forgive.

My flesh is tormented by piteous disease,
And my free spirit already rests, serene.
I remember only the garden, tender, leafless,
    autumnal,
And the black fields and the cry of the
    cranes . . .
Oh, how sweet was the earth for me with
    you!

> July 1916
> Slepnyovo

How I love, how I loved to look
At your chained shores,
At the balconies, where for hundreds of
    years
No one has set foot.
And verily you are the capital
For us who are mad and luminous;
But when that special, pure hour
Lingers over the Neva
And the May wind sweeps
Past all the columns lining the water,
You are like a sinner turning his eyes,
Before death, to the sweetest dream of
    paradise . . .

1916

Oh no, it wasn't you I loved
When I burned with a sweet flame,
So explain, what kind of power
Is there in your sad name?

You knelt before me
As if waiting to be crowned,
And deathly shadows touched
Your peaceful young brow.

And you went off. Not to victory,
To death. Endless nights!
Oh my angel, may you not know, not be
    aware of
My present sorrow.

But if the forest path lights up
With the white sun of paradise,
But if a meadow bird
Soars from the prickly sheaves,

I will know: it is you—killed—
Wanting to tell me about it,
And again I'll see the pockmarked hill
Over the Dniestr's bloody swirl.

I will forget days of love and fame,
I will forget my youth.
The soul is dark, the way is treacherous,
But your image, your righteous deed
I will preserve until the hour of death.

July 19, 1917
Slepnyovo

Isn't it to escape from this damned easy life
That I peer uneasily into dark chambers?
Already accustomed to high, pure chimes,
Already beyond the judgment of earthly laws,
I, like a criminal, am still drawn there,
To that place of slow execution and shame.
And I see a marvelous town, and I hear a
   beloved voice,
As if there were not also a mysterious grave,
Where, day and night, bowing down, in heat
   and cold,
I must await the Judgment Day.

January 1917

You will live without misfortune,
You will govern, you will judge.
With your quiet partner
You will raise your sons.

Success in everything you do,
From everyone respect and praise,
You won't know that I, from crying,
Lose track of the days.

There are many of us homeless ones,
And our strength is
That for us, benighted and blind,
The house of God shines.

And for us, descending into the vale,
The altars burn,
And our voices soar
To God's very throne.

1915

I will tend these rich, black beds,
With spring water I will sprinkle them;
The flowers of the field are free,
There's no need to touch or pick them.

Let them be more plentiful than stars
    kindled
In the September skies—
For children, for wanderers, for lovers
They grow, those wild flowers.

But mine—are for Saint Sophia
On that one bright day
When prayers and responses
Soar from beneath the marvelous canopy.

And, as the waves wash to the shore
That which they themselves condemned to
    death,
I bring my penitential soul
And flowers from the Russian earth.

Summer 1916
Slepnyovo

I brought disaster to my dear ones,
And one after another they died.
Oh, woe is me! These graves
Were foretold by my words.
Like circling crows smelling
Hot, fresh blood
Were those savage songs
Sent by my exultant love.

With you it is sweet and sultry,
You are close as the heart in my breast.
Give me your hands, listen carefully.
I'm warning you: Go away.

And let me not know where you are.
O Muse, don't call him,
Let him live unsung,
Unaware of my love.

August 1921
Petersburg

Some of them exchange fond glances,
Others drink until the sun's first rays,
But all night I negotiate
With my indomitable conscience.

I say: "I've been carrying your
Heavy burden, you know, for so many
    years."
But for it, time does not exist,
And for it there is no space.

Once again there's the black, Carnival night,
The sinister park, the horse's deliberate pace,
And the wind filled with happiness and
    gaiety
Swooping down on me from heaven's height.

But when that special, pure hour
Lingers over the Neva
And the May wind sweeps
Past all the columns lining the water . . .

Now no one will listen to songs.
The prophesied days have begun.

And over me a tranquil, two-horned
Witness stands . . . Oh there, there,
Along the ancient road under the Caprice,
Where there are swans and dead still water.

November 3, 1935

Fountain House

## NUMBER THREE, ZACHATEVSKY

A side street, a side str . . .
Stretched like a noose around your neck.

It drags coolness from the Moscow River,
In its windows little lights glimmer.

There on the left hand—vacant lots,
And on the right hand—a monastery,

And opposite—a giant maple tree
That listens to long groans at night.

The rotting lamppost leans—
The bell ringer leaves the tower . . .

I wish I could find that little icon,
Because my time is near.

I'd like my black shawl again,
I'd like a drink of Neva water.

1940

. . . And the man who means
Nothing to me now, but was my concern
And comfort in the bitterest years—
Wanders like a ghost on the outskirts,
The back streets and the back yards of life,
Heavy, stupefied by insanity,
With a wolfish grin . . .
    O God, God, God!
In your eyes how grievously I have sinned!
Leave me pity at least . . .

January 13, 1945

I bid farewell to everyone,
And on the day of Christ's Resurrection,
Those who betrayed me I kiss on the brow,
And those who did not—on the lips.

In every tree, the crucified Lord,
The body of Christ in every ear of grain,
And prayer's immaculate word
Heals fleshly pain.

1946

# THE HEIRESS

It seemed to me that a song rang out
Through these empty halls.
Oh, who could have told me back then
That I would inherit it all:
Felitsa, the bridges, the swans,
And all the Chinese fantasies,
The palace's long galleries
And the wonderful beauty of the linden
trees.

And even my own shade,
All distorted by fear,
And the shirt of repentance
And the lilac by the grave.

November 20, 1959<br>Leningrad

# THE LAST ONE

I delighted in deliriums,
In singing about tombs.
I distributed misfortunes
Beyond anyone's strength.
The curtain not raised,
The circle dance of shades—
Because of that, all my loved ones
Were taken away.
All this is disclosed
In the depths of the roses.
But I am not allowed to forget
The taste of the tears of yesterday.

1964

The violent wine of lechery
They have drunk to the lees.
They don't see the pure face of truth
And the tears of repentance they don't
   recognize.

Stop it, I was like all of them,
And worse than all of them.
I bathed in someone else's dew
And I hid in someone else's oatfield,
On someone else's grass I slept.

LIBRARY OF CONGRESS
CATALOGING-IN-PUBLICATION DATA

Akhmatova, Anna Andreevna, 1889–1966.
    [Poems. English. Selections]
    A stranger to heaven and earth: poems of Anna Akhmatova/
translated and edited by Judith Hemschemeyer.
    —1st Shambhala ed.    p.    cm.—(Shambhala Centaur
Editions)
    ISBN 0-87773-894-7 (alk. paper)
    1. Akhmatova, Anna Andreevna, 1889–1966—Translations
into English.    I. Hemschemeyer, Judith.    II. Title.    III. Series
PG3476.A324A234    1993    93-20170
891.71'42—dc20    CIP

SHAMBHALA CENTAUR EDITIONS are named for a classical modern typeface designed by the eminent American typographer Bruce Rogers. Modeled on a fifteenth-century Roman type, Centaur was originally an exclusive titling font for the Metropolitan Museum of Art, New York. The first book in which it appeared was Maurice de Guérin's *The Centaur*, printed in 1915. Until recently, Centaur type was available only for handset books printed on letterpress. Its elegance and clarity make it the typeface of choice for Shambhala Centaur Editions, which include outstanding classics of the world's literary and spiritual traditions.

SHAMBHALA CENTAUR EDITIONS

Back to Beginnings: Reflections on the Tao
*by Huanchu Daoren*
*Translated by Thomas Cleary*

Dewdrops on a Lotus Leaf: Zen Poems of Ryokan
*Translated by John Stevens*

For Love of the Dark One: Songs of Mirabai
*Translated by Andrew Schelling*
*Illustrated by Mayumi Oda*

Look! This is Love: Poems by Rumi
*Translated by Annemarie Schimmel*

Narrow Road to the Interior
*by Matsuo Basho*
*Translated by Sam Hamill*